Dare to Change Life series

A Shift
Toward
Abundance

Secrets to
Financial Freedom

By
Millen Livis, M.S., M.B.A.

Dedication

To Yann, my best friend and true supporter. You helped me achieve many of the milestones in my life and I am forever grateful to you.

Contents

Contents

Contents

Free Bonus
"A Shift Toward Abundance"
Audiobook

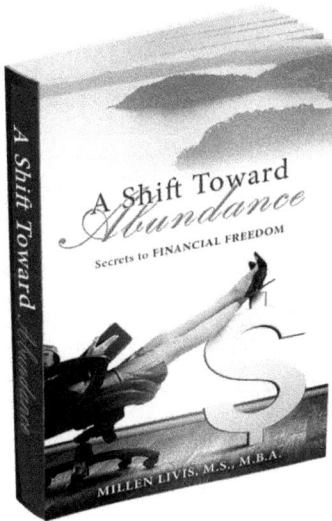

If you'd like to listen to the audiobook version of "A Shift Toward Abundance: Secrets to Financial Freedom" while you follow along with the book or walk or ... drive, you can download it for free for a limited time at **http://millenlivis.com/abundance**

Dare
to Change
Life

Introduction

I find discussions about money, financial freedom and abundance are some of the most desirable as well as the most uncomfortable topics of all. Most people wish to have more of that but many *don't want to talk or learn* about getting *that*...for various perceived reasons like: "It's not possible for me," or "I am not the *money type*."

While there is a growing number of self-help books, TV and Internet talk shows and movies about the law of attraction and manifesting abundance, it appears to me that there is a missing link—a gap in this conversation—*the dual nature of wealth manifestation*: the physical and the metaphysical (spiritual). It is my objective in this book to bridge the gap.

With worldwide national debts exploding, stock markets getting more volatile and high unemployment rates becoming a "new normal," there is a growing need for self-sufficiency, personal responsibility and financial literacy.

More people are becoming aware of the "non-physical" aspects of money and financial freedom, the importance of rising above race, humble origins or challenging circumstances—lack of opportunities or education—in order to achieve goals of financial freedom.

Many people realize now that money is a solidified form of energy and that uplifting your own energy will help you attract "more of the same" and put you in the flow of abundance. That is postulated by one of the universal laws that rules our lives—the law of attraction, also known as the law of resonance.

However, in addition to the metaphysical aspects of attracting wealth, it is important to have the "know-how" tools to create, grow and manage your wealth. There are many documented cases of people who received fortunes by winning lotteries but went back to being poor because they had neither basic knowledge nor skills in order to manage their fortunes.

If you choose to rely on other people for managing your money, prepare to be disappointed if you have no clue as to what they do and why they do it. It is your responsibility to become an educated client. Nobody cares about your money and financial freedom more than you do!

It is my intention in this book to emphasize the importance of both—the metaphysical aspects of money and abundance consciousness as well as the physical, practical "know-how" tools of creating and managing wealth. I want to inspire people to take responsibility for their own finances.

Money doesn't define your worthiness but rather reveals your belief system about yourself and your life. You may choose to view money as a reward for your talents, skills and your contributions to other people's lives. It could also be a fuel by which you transcend your own self-image, realize your vision and express compassion.

Stop worrying about money. Instead, be ready to take advantage of opportunities that come your way, allow abundance to flow freely through you then learn how to grow and manage your wealth. Where you are now in your pursuit of financial freedom is less important than your intention and commitment to achieve it.

Dare
to Change
Life

Abundance Consciousness

"Expect your every need to be met. Expect the answer to every problem, expect abundance on every level...."

~ Eileen Cady

We live in a vibrational world, which means that everything is energy. Your physical body, your thoughts, feelings, material possessions, money, friends and family—all are energy. Most people function on the physical plane—at the level of their five senses—and don't realize the depth and sophisticated design of human existence.

When you think of or talk about money as a necessary evil or something that always eludes you, you unconsciously create experiences in your life that confirm your feelings. On the contrary, if you respect money as a *form of available energy* that enables and reflects opportunities, your actions will be aligned with these feelings and you will create positive money experiences.

The Law of Resonance

A very powerful law that governs the vibration and resonance of this universe—the law of attraction—postulates that you draw to yourself the essence of your predominant attention. When your thoughts are focused on misfortune, scarcity or lack as opposed to abundance, joy and peace, you attract experiences that have the same vibration.

In order to attract something, the vibration of your thoughts and feelings must match the vibration of your desires. You can attract your desire by consistently focusing *on its presence* because the *vibrational frequency of its presence is very different than that of its absence*.

You attract the vibrational equivalence of what YOU emit while placing your attention on something. The more you think about it, the more you vibrate and emit matching energy. Therefore, thinking about something is like planting a seed: when you worry, you seed misfortune; when you appreciate, you seed success.

Your Relationship with Money

Each of us develops a *relationship with money*. Most people learn fearful, negative beliefs about money from their environment—family members, friends and media propaganda. The messages of *scarcity* and *lack* get accepted as true.

Perhaps you received money-demonizing mind programming when you heard that the rich deprive the poor and that when you become wealthy you get disconnected from your higher self, from appreciating truth, goodness and love. Consequently, various books and seminars about abundance often feel like nuisance and hype because they don't resonate with your personal experience.

When having a lot of money is associated with greed, corruption and deception, achieving true abundance is impossible. Perceiving money as a token of energy exchange, a symbol of appreciation and a ticket to a harmonious and fulfilling life will lead everyone to positive money and life experiences.

Abundance is Your Birthright

For centuries, prominent philosophers and religious leaders have taught about our birthright—divine abundance—which flows through everybody's life naturally and freely. The ideas of peace, harmony and abundance are common to all cultures and philosophies. I believe that *abundance consciousness—the belief in your own proficiency to achieve abundance and liberty and the willingness to support others in their pursuit of financial freedom and fulfillment*—is a precursor for experiencing wealth and freedom in your life.

It is exciting to see the amazing abundance of our planet: the enormous variety found in the animal and plant kingdoms, the stars, the oceans and the lushness of life itself. If you choose to see abundance in your life, you'll realize that abundance is natural to you too.

Therefore, I invite you to start reminding yourself that there are trillions of dollars, euros and yens floating around and you can attract wealth by various means like selling your ideas and products, offering important services or learning to invest your money. People are willing to exchange money for *in-demand* products and services.

True abundance cannot be experienced in isolation from other people. If you want to experience divine abundance, you need to find ways to uplift others, to help others strengthen themselves so they too may experience abundance.

Self-empowerment, financial responsibility and gratitude are the most important qualities to be cultivated in order to align yourself with *abundance consciousness* because you need to achieve a *vibrational harmony with what you desire.*

Your Beliefs About Money Rule Your Life

Money is a solidified form of energy and, as such, is completely neutral. Acquiring a lot of money doesn't change people but rather illuminates who they have always been. Money is not evil. What is evil is greed, obsession with power, jealousy and anger. Wealth, when used wisely, can instigate incredible opportunities of generosity, spiritual growth and other positive contributions.

There are times in life when things seem to fall apart. Nowadays, many people are unemployed and live in fear of financial uncertainty. Although you may feel like there is nothing positive in financial hardship, you can choose to see this challenge as an opportunity to change your way of thinking and change the direction of your life. Sometimes people need to experience *no money* moments to get a wake-up call and *do the work* necessary to get back to *abundance consciousness*.

Learning to align yourself with the flow of money and abundance is part of your spiritual journey, your "Earth class" as says Gary Zukav. Humans are creatures of habits: if you find yourself in a pattern of financial predicaments, ask why—and then search for answers that will bring improvement. By doing so, you'll break the cycle and create real change in your life.

I believe that lack of money is not a *curse* or *bad luck* but a sign that mistakes were made, lessons were presented, and an opportunity is open to *correct* the mistakes.

Dare
to Change
Life

Accept Responsibility

"Liberty means responsibility.
That is why most men dread it."
~ George Bernard Shaw

It is my belief that we live in a new Age of Enlightenment—when the ideas of spiritual empowerment, self-sufficiency and personal responsibility for your own life are prevalent. More people realize that accepting responsibility for individual empowerment is the only way to self-liberation.

Unfortunately, there are still many institutions and authorities empowered to act as custodians of society and cover up manipulation, deception and control under the guise of *public interest*. Entitlement mentality, combined with unconditional government-sponsored subsidies and ideas of *wealth redistribution* are examples of the way society exerts power over individuals.

The *pursuit of happiness* is still the goal of all people. Many individuals question the philosophy of *disempowerment and dependency* and realize that the only solution to society's problems is acceptance of personal responsibility for their own values and lives.

Make Responsible Choices

Millions of driven, creative people manage to achieve financial freedom and personal fulfillment despite new rules and regulations, tax increases, and fear-based manipulation of the political system. *When you take full responsibility—without blaming yourself or others—for your life, you empower yourself to change and create the life you want.*

You have a choice: continue to be controlled by your *money drama* or pause, decide and change the course of your life. The latter will let you move confidently toward *your vision.*

Past experiences don't define your future. Once you acknowledge that you and only you are responsible for your *money drama* and allow yourself to move beyond guilt and fear, you can then apply universal laws of money and abundance, learn practical money management tools, raise your self-confidence and put yourself on track for a new life experience—free of guilt, fear, worry or lack.

Nobody is perfect and you learn by the virtue of your mistakes. No matter how humble your beginning may be— dare to dream big and believe that it is possible!

Own Your Decisions

As much as it is important to be aware of your thoughts and feelings, it is equally important to take ownership for all your choices, decisions and actions and assume responsibility for the consequences of your decisions and actions instead of whining, complaining and blaming others.

If you cannot afford to buy a house or a car at the moment—accept it and focus on the things you can afford and can do. Appreciate them wholeheartedly. If you cannot take a dream vacation right now because you are responsible for paying your student loans—accept it and keep your dream alive.

Not being able to have something or experience something at this time in your life doesn't mean that you will never have it or experience it. It simply means that you must be deliberate with your ways of thinking (since you attract what you focus on) and keep being excited but patient about the timing of your dreams.

Accepting your current circumstances, *allowing* yourself to be OK with what you have and what you do and *appreciating* it all will help you release inner tension and stress, avoid envy and self-sabotage and receive that which you desire.

When you were in school, the grade of 'A' meant that your performance was excellent. In the school of Earth, you can put yourself on a similar 'A' program by following the tenets of Accept, Allow and Appreciate:

- **A**ccept your current circumstances
- **A**llow yourself to let go of guilt, shame and comparisons
- **A**ppreciate yourself and your ability to open to new ideas, opportunities and actions

Never Give Up

When you drive a car from point A to point B, you know it takes time to get to point B. You accept the fact that distance and time are aspects of travel. While you may wonder what will happen on the road, you believe in your ability to reach point B.

Although you may encounter a delay or two, discouragement doesn't enter your mind. You accept the effort that this journey requires and continue moving toward your destination.

Your life journey—from where you are now in your life to where you want to be—requires similar confidence, patience and determination. *Your feelings are your inner guidance system.*

Trusting your feelings will help you achieve greater alignment with *abundance consciousness*. If what you feel, do and have brings you an experience of joy, love and harmony then you are moving in the right direction.

Now that you are clear about the dynamics of your *non-physical* existence, shift gears to the nuts and bolts of the physical plane, the money management system, which will guide you on your journey to financial freedom.

CHAPTER 3

Common Sense and Financial Freedom

"A big part of financial freedom is having your heart and mind free from worry about the what-ifs of life."

~ Suze Orman

My desire for financial independence was always stronger than the desire to own anything (e.g. designer clothes, luxurious vacations or fancy cars). I was fortunate enough to have a professional career that allowed me to support my family, accumulate savings and make decent investments, but it didn't provide a way toward financial independence.

My relentless quest for financial freedom and meaningful work led me to becoming an entrepreneur. Leaving a *steady paycheck* job was nerve-racking at first but *it felt right in my body* even though it was not easy. I made mistakes and learned lessons in the process—which is what happens when one dares to change life!

I consider myself a risk-taker, which served me well with a few exceptions, especially in the stock market investment arena. When I was young, reckless and naïve, I wanted to become financially free overnight. Common sense approaches to investment—longer time horizon, rational vs. emotional choice of stocks, diversification as a risk management tool, etc.—were too slow and boring for me.

I used to chase hot tips; loaned money from my house's equity line to a businessman I hardly knew and even invested my entire pension plan in the stock of the company I used to work for. My pension portfolio was performing great...until the stock crashed and I lost almost everything.

As you can see, I was reckless and lacked *common sense* in my investing at that time. As a result of all my mistakes, missteps and lessons learned, I developed three *Financial Freedom Rules:*

1. ***Don't spend more than you earn.***
2. ***Don't borrow more than you can afford.***
3. ***Build multiple streams of income.***

I see a lot of people in our country, some are really smart and well educated, who are so addicted to spending that no matter how much they earn, they manage to spend even more.

There are a few high-paid professionals like investment bankers, executives, doctors and lawyers, who have higher than average compensation and yet are not financially free. Many of these high wage earners incurred massive debt and owe more than they can afford.

They are under enormous stress and have to deal with creditors and mounting debt. Apparently, what is most important is *not just how much they earn but how much they spend.* Is this also true for you?

Don't Spend More Than You Earn

If you are tired of *financial slavery* and currently have a habit of spending more than you earn—have a balance on your credit card, use multiple credit cards, borrow from your house's equity line, etc. —you must cultivate *financial freedom habits* by following this first financial freedom rule.

How? By cutting your spending by 20-50 percent across the board. You can do this by bringing homemade lunches to work; cutting back on restaurant spending; downsizing your lifestyle (trading your expensive house for a modest one); selling a luxury car and buying a good used model; taking low-budget vacations.

Assess your entire budget and create efficient balances between your needs, desires and abilities to pay for things.

You get the idea. Your desire to be financially independent must be stronger than complacency and the "I am broke" mentality. You can break the *financial slavery habits* but you must decide to *change your priorities* and *develop the discipline to buy what you need and can afford,* while still dreaming of what you'd love to be able to create in your life.

Don't Borrow More Than You Can Afford

Having a lot of debt through mortgages, car loans, student loans and credit card balances restricts your choices and limits your opportunities to borrow money to pay for something essential in your life.

Because of the recent real estate crisis in the United States, millions of people got burned because they ended up with *under-water mortgages* when the values of their houses dropped drastically. Most of these homeowners couldn't sell their properties to repay what they owed even if they wanted to. Foreclosures devastated a lot of families that got caught up in the American dream of owning their home, even if they hardly could afford it.

When you borrow money from the bank to buy a new car or a house, you don't *really* own it—the bank owns it until you pay off your loan. What you do own is the loan as well as the responsibility to pay both the balance and the interest rate on the loan.

The *common sense approach* is to *purchase a car* (avoid leasing a car for personal use); *use a debit card* or *pay your credit card bill each month in-full*; *pay cash for assets that don't appreciate over time* (car, appliances, TV); *rent an apartment or a house until you have enough savings to buy it* with a low loan-to-value ratio; *pay for college tuition by using scholarships, grants, job programs or low-cost student loans.*

If you have a lot of debt, work to get your budget to a *'sleep well' point—a position when you can comfortably manage your must-pay* expenses. When that is achieved, then start planning to own assets that are likely to appreciate over time, such as rental properties with a positive cash flow; precious metals (coins and bars); valuable pieces of art; bonds and stock shares issued by established dividend paying companies.

Build Multiple Streams of Income

I like to make financial decisions that support two of my most essential values in life—freedom and peace of mind. I have a sense of calm knowing that even if one of my streams of income faces challenges, I can rely on other streams of income.

It takes time and creative thinking to come up with multiple channels of additional earnings, especially when you work for a company, but it is possible. Look at your passions and talents and offer services that people need, would benefit from and are willing to pay for. Obviously, a decision to create a personal enterprise depends on your individual skills, talents, experience and available time.

Begin by contemplating the very idea of having multiple streams of income. Imagine the peace of mind that it would bring to you... then proceed confidently toward implementing your ideas.

Here are examples of income streams:
- Your main job or business
- Rental real estate properties
- Teaching dance or yoga classes
- Consulting in the area of your expertise

- Freelance writing
- Freelance photography
- Creating an Internet-based business selling products or services
- Becoming a stock market day-trader or investor
- Starting a brick-and-mortar (traditional) business

CHAPTER 4

The Roadmap to Financial Freedom

"If you're not staying on top of your money, you are putting your financial well-being at risk."

~ Suze Orman

You have a relationship with money and it leads to your money habits, which create your money story. Here are some questions for you to contemplate:

1. Do you believe in personal responsibility and financial discipline?
2. Do you habitually shop for what you need or for what you want?
3. Are you willing to reduce your expenses or would you rather incur debt to support your current lifestyle?
4. Do you practice financial discipline when it comes to using a credit card?
5. Do you pay all your bills on time or frequently incur additional interest for deferred or late payments?

6. Do you spend less than what you earn?
7. Do you save a portion of your income for unforeseen circumstances?
8. Do you take time to educate yourself about your investments or just follow your financial advisers?
9. Do you know how to manage financial risk?
10. Do you plan allocation of your income?

Your individual answers to these questions and the *family money story that you recall from your childhood* will provide a fairly accurate picture of your personal *money blueprint.*

Clarity about your money habits and awareness of your current money blueprint will help you realize that it's not your bad luck or generational misfortune that blocks your financial freedom, but rather the choices that you make every day.

If you want to change your money habits, you need to replace them with better ones and practice them consistently. Very few people do it, but those who do, achieve financial freedom. Are you on board?

Prudent Wealth Creation and Wealth Management System

Here are the *Golden Rules of Wealth Creation*:

1. **Don't lose money**
   (be alert and exercise prudence).
2. **Don't spend more than you make**
   (if you have dug yourself into a hole–stop digging).
3. **Don't take risks that make you lose sleep**
   (don't rush into any get-rich-quick schemes).

4. Become a little richer every day/month
   (develop a *wealth growth* pattern).
5. Cultivate and maintain discipline with your wealth creation efforts.

You may perceive these rules as symbolic, obvious or unrealistic. I suggest that you internalize and apply them. In order to successfully grow and manage your wealth, create a structure and discipline to maintain it.

Organizing your money based on purpose (saving, spending, investing), your risk tolerance and timeline will allow you to avoid feeling scared and overwhelmed and will give you peace of mind and clarity.

To make my point, think of a *jar* as a money container (obviously, money isn't really kept in *jars* but rather in bank accounts, brokerage accounts, credit unions accounts, coins and property/land.) Keeping all your money together in one big *jar* could lead to a financially devastating decision.

Although dividing your money among different categories may not preclude you from making mistakes, maintaining the discipline of adhering to this structure will help you limit your losses and avoid financial ruin.

Imagine that your future income is located deep in the ground, in a *money mine*, and you first need to extract it—apply efforts to earn it—then divide it into the following three *jars*:

1. Spending—money exchanged for shelter, food, services and pleasure.
2. Saving—money that stays in place as a foundation.

3. Investing—money used in order to grow your wealth.

The objective is to fill all three *money jars*, which is equivalent to achieving your goal of financial freedom. Although this goal may seem unrealistic at first, especially for those with a modest single income source, it is up to you when to start. Trust yourself to know the best time to begin your path to financial freedom. My advice is to start as soon as possible because it takes time to accumulate wealth.

CHAPTER 5

Spending

"Never spend your money before you have earned it."

~ Thomas Jefferson

This prudent Wealth Creation and Management System is simple, easy to practice and it works. It requires your desire to win the money game, a bit of common sense and a commitment to stay the course. This system will abolish your money drama and allow you to live well now and in the future.

As a first generation immigrant to America, I experienced a modest lifestyle after arriving. Although well educated, my family had a very humble beginning in this country. I was happy about every work opportunity, even the minimum wage jobs I had, because it was an opportunity to take care of my family's needs.

During that time we were spending 80 percent of the money we earned on necessities (food, clothing, transportation, job searches) but we never felt poor. Although we worked hard just to make ends meet, we enjoyed quality time with family and friends, felt blessed for the opportunity to live in a great country and were inspired to achieve *financial freedom*.

Whatever your current income may be, you can plan for spending in such a way that would allow you to live comfortably and enjoy life. The opposite of this kind of *positive spending* is *wasteful spending*, leading to depletion and lack. Wasteful spending is also involved when you are carrying the burden of high risk (as in buying into get-rich-quick schemes).

The truth about money is interesting! You can enjoy life on a modest income and yet feel miserable while making a fortune. Your family can be just as happy in a $300,000 house as in a house valued at $3,000,000 million. Driving a decent used car will get you to your destination the same way as a new one but you will not lose money for paying a premium to drive the *latest season model*. Dining at home more often than at a restaurant allows you to have quality homemade food and to save money.

You can create a stylish look by having fewer, better quality clothes, and learning how to put them together in a way that embellishes your appearance. You can find great vacation opportunities on a relatively small budget—just research on the Internet. Many luxuries can be discovered for very little money. Challenge yourself to find them, then enjoy the surprise.

Whatever you want to buy, do it because YOU want it and can afford it, not to impress family members, neighbors or colleagues. Owning expensive things is far less important than having an attentive, compassionate and kind personality.

It is very difficult to accumulate wealth and achieve financial freedom if your *spending appetite* increases every time your income goes up. Your *spending money jar* has a hole in it... everything you put in it will be gone by the end of the year unless you can re-fill it as fast as you spend it.

Be mindful of your spending appetite. Setting very aggressive financial goals or desiring and acquiring *expensive toys*—fancy new cars, extravagant vacations, exquisite jewelry, etc.—drives many smart folks to take greater risks.

Some very successful people experience financial ruin by taking too much risk—spending faster than earning. When it comes to wealth building, spending money conservatively is the key.

Annual Spending Rate Calculation

I invite you to discover two steps to creating a *spending strategy*—one that allows you to live your *best life,* free from financial stress and filled with possibilities and joy.

Step 1: Determine the *size* of your *spending jar*— your Annual Spending Rate (ASR). Take some time and, using an Excel spreadsheet, list the 12 months of the year along the side and make two columns at the top:

1. Must-Have—Must-Pay

2. *Nice-to-Have—Choose-to-Pay*

Now, enter your *necessary* monthly expenses into the *Must-Have—Must-Pay* column: rent, food, clothes, transportation, utilities, medical insurance, student loans, taxes, etc.

Next, enter your arbitrary monthly expenses into the *Nice-to-Have—Choose-to-Pay* column: phone, computer, car, gas, transportation, insurance, TV subscription, entertainment, eating out, clothing, etc.

Step 2: Add all monthly amounts from these two columns. This total amount is your ASR.

Once you have your ASR number, make sure that your *Nice-to-Have–Choose-to-Pay* amount doesn't increase every year!

If you truly want to achieve financial freedom, you must know your ASR in order to be aware of your spending habits. Your monthly spending rate is very important but I suggest calculating the ASR because there are some annual expenses like home insurance, car insurance and taxes.

Bottom line: make your *spending money jar* big enough to be able to enjoy life but small enough to allow you to fill your *saving and investing money jars* fairly quickly.

CHAPTER 6

Saving

*"Don't tell me where your priorities are. Show
me where you spend your money and I'll tell
you what they are."*

~ James W. Frick

Once you calculate your annual spending requirement,
you can start focusing on your saving and investment
money jars. When you are at the beginning of your career
and just entering the self-sufficient life phase, you may not
have a lot of money left after your spending allocation.

I invite you to make your best effort to put some money
aside for your *saving money jar*. It will teach you to be
more disciplined with your *spending* and help you develop
healthy *money habits*.

Your *saving money jar's* purpose is to provide you with
peace of mind while you grow your wealth. When you
have savings, you avoid becoming stressed out about
your *Must-Have—Must-Pay* commitments and needs in
case you lose your main source of income.

The idea is to put aside a portion of your current
earnings to cover your needs in case of financial adversity

like sudden unemployment or illness/disability and short-term, up-coming situations such as loan pay-downs or pay-offs, car or home repairs. Thus, your *savings money* must be safe and liquid—meaning easy to access.

I suggest that you start putting aside funds to save for the following:

1. **Emergency fund**—up to 12 months' worth of your *Must-Have—Must-Pay* spending money amount.

2. **Short Term fund**—discretionary amount of money for something that you expect to pay for within two to five years, such as a new car, a down payment on a house, a college tuition or vacation.

Your **emergency fund** must be absolutely safe—your objective with this money is to preserve capital, not to grow it. This money is to be kept as super-safe to maintain value and very liquid. Given today's economy, your savings could be apportioned among the following *asset types*:

- Cash (savings account with a small interest rate)
- Physical gold and silver bullion or coins
- Treasury notes—two, three, five or ten years U.S. debt obligations that are sold by the U.S Treasury Department and secured by the U.S. government

The way in which you choose to save your money is important. Allocating your super-safe funds across different kinds of assets (e.g. cash, bullion, notes) is called **diversification**.

Diversifying your money decreases the risk of losing the value of your money at once. The old saying "don't put all your eggs in the same basket" is wise and reminds you about risk management.

Having *emergency fund* money is extremely important. Imagine for a brief moment that you've lost your job and need to liquidate your stock portfolio to cover your *Must-Have—Must-Pay* expenses. Then you realize that your investment portfolio has lost its value because of poor stock market performance ... or worse, a market crash.

Unfortunately, a scenario like that is very real and has 'burned' many people. Your safe *emergency fund* money will allow you to cover your expenses until you find another job or find a new stream of income.

Your **short term fund**—*discretionary money*—can be held in safe, fairly conservative investment vehicles like these:

- High-investment grade corporate bonds
- High-interest, FDIC-insured bank CDs
- Market-safe FDIC-insured CDs, which fluctuate with the market but guarantee your principal investment
- Common stock of well-established international companies that have healthy balance sheets (low debt obligation and a lot of cash saved) and a long history of dividend payments to their shareholders
- Tax-free safe municipal bonds (not all municipalities' bonds are safe—do your research)

When your timeline for using these funds gets close to two years away (say you have a debt obligation to fulfill)—reallocate this *short term fund's* capital into safer investments, like those in *emergency fund*.

Your objective with the *savings money jar* is absolute, positive risk aversion. You can compensate low Return On Investment (ROI) in this fund by riskier but higher ROI investments in your *investment money* jar.

Emergency Fund and Short Term Fund Calculations

Determine the size of your *emergency fund*—12 month safe-savings *survival fund*. This should be fairly easy since you already calculated your ASR (annual spending rate). Therefore, you already have your *Must-Have—Must-Pay* amount and *Nice-to-Have—Choose-to-Pay* calculations ready. All you need to do is to add the most important items from the *Nice-to-Have—Choose-to-Pay* list of expenses to your *Must-Have—Must-Pay* expense amount.

To calculate your *short term* fund, add all your upcoming debt obligations (mortgage down payment or tuition amount, cost of a new car, etc.) and retirement contributions. It is expected that you may not know all your short-term upcoming needs at this moment. Thus, simply keep this calculation up-to-date as your situation changes.

CHAPTER 7

Investing

"It is human nature to think wisely and act in an absurd fashion."

~ Anatole France

The purpose of your investing money jar is to grow your wealth over a longer term, for example, over a five year period. This investing money jar is usually meant for retirement funds, children's college expenses, or long-term dreams, such as a owning a second home or leisure travel.

Since your *investing jar* has a longer timeline, it is important to find investment vehicles that yield a nice rate of return or ROI, a steady 8 to 15 percent annual return. Personally, I like investments that are *valued cheap*, are *hated at the present time* and have *started to rise*. Examples from the past: real estate properties in 2011, precious metals in 2001-2004, stocks in the spring of 2009.

Diversify Your Sources of Income

If you're starting your investment strategy from scratch, the earlier you start investing with even mediocre interest rates, the faster your wealth will grow. Even small but consistent contributions will fill your *investing money jar* faster.

Multiple streams of income allow you to grow your wealth faster and provide an additional sense of security due to *diversification.* Having *multiple streams of income* is one of the main secrets of acquiring wealth.

The ultimate goal is to be able to provide a comfortable living for yourself and your family from each individual stream of income. This is a much more prudent way to achieve wealth than getting into risky investments. The idea here is to leverage your skills, experiences, inner wisdom and hobbies to expand your earning potentials.

Risk Management Practices

The most important question to ask when considering any investment opportunity is "How much money can I lose?" Being a successful investor requires patience and caution. Since I am not naturally wired with these faculties, I have to make a conscious effort to pause and ask myself these *risk management* questions:

1. How much can I lose if things do not work out as I hope?
2. How can I minimize the amount of loss?

Asking these questions gives me time to contemplate risk management tactics and helps get my emotions out of the way. Once I take care of the potential risk, then I can focus on the fun part—making money!

Most people who are new to investing are focused on the potential upside, chasing the latest *hot opportunity*. They are not inclined to think about what would happen if the best-case scenario *doesn't* happen (and it rarely does). Every person has a different *risk tolerance*, but investors who employ prudent risk management strategies usually enjoy steady wealth growth and experience much less worry and stress.

Longer Term Investment Timeline Decreases Risk

Trading does not equate to investing. There are a lot of day-traders—people who trade in-and-out within few days by taking advantage of short-term market fluctuations. Very few short-term or day traders have acquired great wealth.

Investing, on the other hand, has a much longer time horizon and most asset classes—stocks, real estate, commodities—appreciate over a longer period of time. This is one more reason to research your investment choices very thoroughly and apply simple risk management approaches.

Furthermore, there are times when *sitting tight/ doing nothing* is the best solution—don't feel pressured to always buy or sell. It's not the frequency of investing but rather the quality of your decisions over time that adds up to great wealth. Learn when to act and when to wait.

Asset Allocation and Diversification As Risk Management

Prudent investing is about reducing risk first. Next it is about managing profits. Nobody can be *right* all the time, and a disciplined attitude coupled with fundamental risk management are essential. Taking on more risk often leaves you feeling broke instead of wealthy.

Asset allocation is an investment strategy that helps balance risk versus reward by adjusting the percentage of each asset in an investment portfolio according to your risk tolerance, goals and investment timeline.

Asset allocation is based on the principle that different assets, not perfectly correlated, perform differently in different economic and market conditions. For example, a conservative portfolio may contain the following asset allocation: 40 percent corporate bonds, 10 percent treasury notes, 20 percent cash, 20 percent precious metals, 10 percent stocks. In contrast, aggressive portfolio may have 100 percent of its funds invested in stocks....

Diversifying your *savings* among different asset classes (cash, bonds, precious metals, etc.) decreases your risk of massive losses. Diversification as a risk management tool is extremely important for choosing the actual investment vehicles.

NEVER... EVER put all or even most of your money in any one particular investment.

If your employer offers you shares of common stock of the company as a form of retirement contribution in addition to your own retirement contributions (a good idea since your contribution is tax free), find out how you can *diversify* all retirement money among different investment vehicles.

Position Sizing Helps Prevent Big Losses

Keeping the discipline of putting no more than 5 percent of your portfolio in one particular position helps avoid significant losses in your asset portfolio. This applies to any asset class.

Imagine putting all of your retirement savings into stock issued by the company where you work…and then watching the stock decline due to conditions beyond the company's control. This imaginary scenario became a reality for a lot of employees during past stock market meltdowns and individual companies' stocks crashes.

Another investment mistake that pertains to position sizing is *price leveraging*. Let's say you purchased 500 shares of a company "Z" at $50/share. Then the stock price falls to $30/share and you decide to buy another 500. Your average cost per share of stock now is $40 and you own 1,000 shares.

In one week the stock "Z" falls further, to $10/share. You decide to take advantage of yet another bargain and buy 1,000 shares more, so your average cost per share becomes $25. It is highly possible that the stock price will continue sliding and you may end up with a disproportionally high amount of bad investment….

I emphasize the importance of having discipline about position sizing and diversification so that you will never end up with disproportionally high amount of bad investments. Greed and emotions are worth enemies when it comes to investment.

Samples of Different Investment Vehicles

Below are a few investment vehicles to consider for your *Investing money* that are diversified among different asset classes:

- **Stock Market: Stocks**—common or preferred shares of corporate stocks (I like steady 'dividend growers'); priced in real time
- **Stock Market: Stock Options**—learn about selling puts and covered calls, otherwise, stay away from option trading
- **Stock Market: Mutual Funds**—a basket of different companies' stocks or bonds; priced daily unlike stocks; often have high management fees
- **Stock Market: Exchange Traded Funds** (EFTs)— also a basket of stocks, commodities or currencies; do not charge management fees; traded like stocks
- **Stock Market: Bonds**—government guaranteed or corporate bonds; pay interest to debt holders (make sure you research the grade of the bonds)
- **Stock Market: Municipal Bonds**—issued by municipalities; many are tax-free and offer a nice interest rate but you must research the solvency of the municipality

- **Stock Market: Annuities**—variable or fixed annuities; could be a great instrument for a retirement investment but most have high management fees and "small font" riders—pay attention and read carefully!
- **Rental Real Estate**—only properties with *positive cash flow* which means rental income is higher than all expenses
- **Private Businesses**—passive or active ownership interest in private businesses (make sure you have proper legal agreements that protect your rights and address your tax liability)
- **Different Currencies Investment**—diversifying your cash holdings among different currencies (can use currency ETFs or find banks that allow you to hold money in different currencies)
- **Art Collection**—make sure you know the value of your art pieces and their potential for appreciation over time
- **Precious Metal Coins: gold, silver, platinum**—these are "real money" and are both investment and insurance vehicles

These are just examples of various asset allocations to consider. You will do just fine with diversifying among few asset classes. However, make sure that within each of the suggested investment classes you further diversify your holdings. For instance, have different stock positions (do not invest more than 5 percent of your stock market portfolio in one particular stock or bond) or different pieces of rental real estate.

Become an Educated Investor

Invest in areas that you have some level of expertise in or be *willing to educate yourself.* You can subscribe to investment newsletters, read books on investing or attend investment seminars.

If you choose to delegate growing your wealth to a financial planner or an investment advisor, research their suggestions and their track record *before* signing up to do business with them. Make sure that advisors are not compensated based on the amount of money you invest with them (not commission-based.)

ALWAYS REMEMBER THIS: Nobody cares about YOUR MONEY more than you do, therefore, exercise extreme caution if you outsource managing your money to others.

Don't Let a Small Loss Become a Huge One

You must exercise utmost discipline with your investments on the stock market because it is extremely difficult to recover your portfolio from a big loss. Here is a market portfolio loss/recovery forecast:

- If you lose 10 percent, you need an 11 percent gain to get back to 'square one'

- If you lose 50 percent, you need a 100 percent gain just to get you back to where you started

You may think it's very unlikely to lose so much on the stock market…and I say it is highly probable and, in fact, happens all the time. Unfortunately, inexperienced investors get *frozen* when they experience high losses of value and do nothing with the hope to at least recover their losses. Most of the time, this *waiting* strategy leads to an even more desperate situation. You don't want this to happen to you!

Experienced investors know that both, the buy and sell decisions are equally important. However, most individual investors are consumed only by decisions about what and when to buy and almost never think about when to sell. Lack of an exit strategy leaves a big gap in successful investing and often leads to losing money on even initially good investments.

You can set a *mental sell stop* for your investment and execute it when your position *hits* this price or enter it explicitly on your brokerage account as a *stop limit* or a *trailing stop. The latter* allows your investment to rise but activates a sell order if the position falls by a preset amount or percentage. This discipline is yet another form of risk management.

As John Maynard Keynes famously noted: "The market can stay irrational longer than you can stay solvent." I suggest that you use limit stops or, better yet, 15 to 25 percent trailing stops on ALL your portfolio positions and apply these stops as soon as you execute your *buy* order. This will limit your losses and preserve your capital, which is the most important thing in investment.

Cool Attitude Factor

It is quite common for novice investors to get emotionally attached to a particular investment and get completely *frozen* and desperate when a *promising investment* starts melting away. That is why a *cool attitude factor*—your temperament—is so essential for successful investing. A high level of stress associated with investments is a sign of an amateur or a greedy attitude.

A poor investor has a "how much can I make on this and how fast?" attitude. A good investor contemplates what needs to be done to minimize losses to pre-set minimums in case the promise of a particular investment doesn't actualize/materialize. Having a disciplined and rational approach instead of a greedy and emotional one with all your investments is absolutely essential to achieving success in investing.

Many times it is smarter to do nothing. Often, just a few wise decisions over time add up to great wealth. Of course, you have to know when to act and with how much.

Compound Interest

I hope by now you've realized that you need to consistently invest as much as possible based on your circumstances.

Another reason your wealth will grow faster with consistent contributions is the *magic of compound interest*. The idea of compound interest goes back to Albert Einstein who famously said: "Compound interest is the eighth wonder of the world. He who understands it, earns it … he who doesn't … pays it."

Compound interest, which is commonly used in finance and economics, occurs when you pay or receive an interest on the sum of principal and interest amounts, not just the initial principal. Simple interest is when the interest is not added to the principal when it gets calculated.

The ultimate result of compounding depends on the *compounding frequency* (e.g. monthly, quarterly, annually). For any given interest rate and compounding frequency, an *equivalent* rate for any different *compounding frequency* exists.

For example, the yearly rate for a loan with 1 percent compound interest per month is approximately 12.68 percent per annum as opposed to 12 percent if it were simple interest. This equivalent yearly rate is often referred to as annual percentage rate (APR).

Compound interest is your friend when you receive it and your enemy when you have to pay it because it grows exponentially. If you currently have or ever had a student loan, a credit card debt or a mortgage on a house, you've paid compound interest.

As it may pertain to your particular investment accounts, always re-invest your accrued interest into additional shares so that compound interest will help grow your investment portfolio. If you use brokerage services like Ameritrade, E-trade or Fidelity Investments, they have an automatic reinvestment option that you can set up online for your brokerage account.

Dare
to Change
Life

Debt

"Borrowing and spending is not the way to prosperity."
~ Paul Ryan

Before you buy anything or incur any expense, ask yourself these two questions:

- How much does it cost?
- Can I afford it?

Having debt can be very dangerous and extremely stressful. Yet it is widespread and sometimes even encouraged in our society.

When banks give you a loan despite your poor credit rating, or credit card companies allow you to carry over balances, or colleges make arrangements for you to obtain student loans that will cover your out-of-control tuition, they don't do it "for you" but rather "to you." They don't do it because you are an honest and deserving person. It's strictly business and a profitable one.

Is Debt a Necessary Evil?

There are a few occasions in life when debt may be useful: when buying a house that you can afford, or buying rental properties that have positive cash flow, or obtaining a reasonable student loan for a profession that requires formal educational credentials.

However, most of the time, debt is unnecessary and often dangerous. It is unnecessary because there are often more gradual and less expensive ways to get what you want. It is dangerous because it often becomes a downward spiral, a 'catch 22' that ruins your health, your relationships and your overall wellbeing.

Remember that in case of a mortgage, a credit card debt, a student loan or a car loan, the interest that you pay is compound interest.

Often children and parents spend a lot of money on college education. But graduates often end up struggling with finding jobs in the current economy and cannot afford to repay the debt of both tuition and compound interest charges. Incurring debt for education must be seriously considered on the basis of your personal situation. A college education may not result in a high-paying job or even guaranteed income.

Debt Rules of Engagement

When you borrow money to buy a car, a house, or furniture, make sure that

- you can afford it and
- the return you are getting on the borrowed money is higher than the cost of borrowing it

The bankers, investment advisors and many politicians don't want you to be afraid of debt, they want you to embrace and be comfortable with it because it is profitable for them!

If you want to achieve financial freedom, here are a few ideas for you to consider and implement:

1. **Avoid debt as much as possible**. Before you decide to buy anything and take on any debt, ask yourself: "How much does it cost?" "Do I REALLY need it now?" and "Can I afford it?"

2. **Use a debit card instead of credit card.** If you don't have enough money on your bank account, you won't be able to purchase.

3. **Pay off full amounts monthly**. If you prefer to use a credit card to take advantage of accumulated points (e.g. airline mileage, dining and shopping discounts), link your credit card to your checking account and set it up in such a way that you'll pay the full amount owed each month and never pay the high interest on the carry-over balances.

4. **Don't lease a car, buy it instead.** Buy a car you can afford, not a car to show off. Avoid borrowing money when buying a car. The car is a depreciating asset and you will pay interest on something that loses value every year.

5. **Prioritize—Pay off your most expensive debt first**. For instance, if you have a credit card debt with 19 percent interest—make paying it off your highest priority, even before allocating money into *savings* and *investment jars*.

6. **Pay off your mortgage and your student loans as fast as possible**. Find out whether there is no penalty for pre-paying your loans (paying a larger amount each payment or paying it twice a month). Paying your mortgage sooner will help you save thousands because of compound interest.

7. **Pay off your less expensive debt while saving and investing**. If you have only less expensive debt left (e.g. low interest student loan debt vs. high interest rate credit card debt) you may still be able to put money aside for your *saving* and *investment money jars*. Also, a return on your savings needs to be just enough to cover the rate of inflation. (Inflation is the rate at which the prices for goods and services increase each year, excluding real estate and gasoline).

Living in fear of bill collectors and feeling overwhelmed about mounting debt is not the life you were meant to live. You can do much, much better! Once you make a decision to change your priorities, become financially free and cultivate simple and healthy *money habits,* you will be, without a doubt, on your way to financial freedom.

CHAPTER 9

Mindset of Scarcity vs. Sufficiency

"When we live in the context of sufficiency,
we find a natural freedom and integrity."
~ Lynne Twist

The mindset of scarcity is wildly spread among people of all walks of life, from folks who live paycheck-to-paycheck to people with large fortunes who worry about losing it all and are crippled by fears and stress.

Most of the time, people inherit the mindset of scarcity from family and friends and from society's culture of "deficiency," "there is not enough" and "more is better." Majority of people are unaware of the ways the scarcity-mentality affects their lives and relationship with money.

When you believe in the notion of scarcity, you focus on *deficiency* in your life and put all your efforts into overcoming the perceived *lack*. Your "chase for more," especially when it comes to money, becomes your guiding objective, your drive, your intention and … your curse. It drains your energy, brings worry and stress into your life and deprives you of joyful and peaceful experiences.

I realize that it is not easy to avoid focusing on scarcity when you are out of a job, have increasing student loan debt or cannot afford to go on vacation with your family. I get it. I've been there. That's why I want you to keep your head high, be honest with yourself about *money issues* but relentlessly believe in your ability to handle any challenges that come your way and have enough patience and wisdom to appreciate the opportunities in your life.

What Do You Choose?

Like with everything in life, you can choose to:
a. Continue crippling your life by fears and insecurities of the scarcity mindset and society's money culture.
b. Expand your ways of seeing life, let go of greed and worry; accept the uncertain nature of life, learn ways to grow wealth and focus your intention on experiencing fulfillment, love and joy.

Once you let go of the paralyzing fear of "not enough," you'll experience a liberating and empowering sense of sufficiency, which comes from knowing that no matter what, *there is enough* and that *you are enough* and *capable of handling any life challenges.*

A Shift in Perception

A sense of *sufficiency* has nothing to do with how much money you have but rather how you relate to money. Some rich people have been crushed in the race for more and have eluded the sense of life fulfillment.

I like what Lynne Twist wrote in her book *The Soul of Money*: "Sufficiency resides inside of each of us and we can call it forward. It is a consciousness, an attention, an intentional choosing of the way we think about our circumstances. In our relationship with money, it is using money in a way that expresses our integrity; using it in a way that *expresses* value rather than *determines* value."

There is a deep sense of satisfaction in earning money, being able to provide for yourself and your family and feeling financially independent. The ultimate success is earning a living by doing what you enjoy, being compensated for the work that uses your creative talents and that you feel passionate about.

When you perceive life from a place of fullness and gratitude, from a place of "having enough and being enough," you experience peace, joy and abundance that money can't buy.

Dare
to Change
Life

Abundance and Freedom

"In the long run, we shape our lives, and we shape ourselves. The process never ends until we die. And the choices we make are ultimately our own responsibility."

~ Eleanor Roosevelt

Among many things, money is a language we use to express the best in us and the worst in us. Your pursuit of wealth and experience of abundance may reflect your intention to feel free and fulfilled, to communicate love and empowerment to others and to express kindness and generosity toward the less fortunate.

Conversely, the pursuit of more money can be driven by various forms of fear—anger, insecurity, jealousy, or revenge. The latter often leads to disappointments, victim mentality and comparisons.

Be inspired by possibilities. Choose to see them. Act assertively to realize them.

Abundance

Seeing abundance all around you and experiencing it inside your body takes discipline and practice. Making time for stillness; quieting your mind by meditating and visualizing your amazing abundant life will help you get into a vibrational state that is aligned with infinite possibilities, prosperity and abundance.

On my website, I offer MP3 recordings of guided visualizations for having an "Optimal Life" and "Creating Your Reality."

One of my favorite self-help authors, Stuart Wilde, writes in his book *The Little Money Bible*: "Once you get real, all your energy can go toward becoming what you really need and want to become. That transformation must be part of your story in this lifetime. Making money is not enough—you will have to do something that has meaning."

Freedom

I am a real worshiper of freedom—personal and financial. It is my belief that you cannot have one without the other. Having wealth doesn't guarantee you personal freedom. Conversely, having personal freedom without financial independence hinders your ability to have a joyful, fulfilling life.

This book is my invitation to you to cultivate a financial freedom attitude. Developing an appreciation for building wealth, practicing financial discipline as well as the mindset of sufficiency will get you to this worthy goal.

A person with the *financial freedom attitude* values freedom more than material possessions, is uncomfortable with having debt and appreciates saving and investing. A person with a *financial slavery attitude* values possessions more than financial independence; is not worried about accumulating debt and spends carelessly.

From my own practice of *abundance consciousness* and the quest for personal and financial freedom, I've compiled a '*big picture' list* of guidelines (see below) that I follow and invite you to do the same on your journey.

10 Guidelines for Achieving Financial Freedom

1. **Take control and assume full responsibility for your money and your financial goals.** Learn practical money management tools and financial discipline.

2. **Follow the Financial Freedom rules.** Spend less, earn more, owe less, get creative about finding additional streams of income.

3. **Eliminate debt as soon as possible.** Start with the one that has the highest interest rate. Be aware of compound interest that you pay upon borrowing.

4. **Strive to have multiple streams of income.** This is a cornerstone of financial security and independence.

5. **Develop discipline by growing your *money jars*—spending, saving and investing.**

6. **Don't trust empty promises.** Don't let people convince you to invest with them. Do your own thorough due-diligence and see the value of the investment yourself. Past performance is not a reason to take chances with *your* money.

7. **Invest in what you know or learn about the area of your investment.** For example, real estate, precious metals, stock market.

8. **Learn about risk management practices**. These include diversification, asset allocation, position allocation, time horizon.

9. **Pay attention to the economic environment**. Identify and ride the waves of the rising market; be aware of forming bubbles (e.g. internet stocks in the late 1990-s, real estate in 2007); get out before bubbles burst. All markets are cyclical; whatever goes up must go down.

10. **Live rich! Notice, enjoy and appreciate the abundance in your everyday life.** Most of what you need to be happy doesn't cost much. Your feelings create your experiences including those related to wealth. *Set your intentions from the place of sufficiency; strive for what you believe in, act confident.*

My suggestions are intended to help, not overwhelm you with ideas that may feel uncomfortable. Find out what works specifically for you. If some of these ideas are new, challenge yourself to learn more!

Take small steps if you must, examine your money habits and start cultivating abundance consciousness. I want you to realize that financial freedom is achievable regardless of where you begin as long as you have a strong desire to be free.

About the Author

Millen Livis is a courage ignitor and possibilities catalyst. She works with women who want to manifest abundance and financial freedom in their lives. She manifested an incredibly blessed life and lives the principles that she teaches.

An author, entrepreneur and wealth coach, Millen helps clients create and live the highest vision for their life and work; develop an abundance mindset and attain financial 'know-how'. With her science and business education, corporate and entrepreneurial background, money management expertise, mindfulness practices and transformational coaching experience, Millen has a unique ability to guide and support clients in achieving extraordinary success in their lives.

http://www.DareToChangeLife.com
http://www.MillenLivis.com
https://www.facebook.com/DareToChangeLife
https://twitter.com/Dare2ChangeLife
https://www.linkedin.com/in/DareToChangeLife

Other books in the

Dare to Change Life series

A Shift Toward Optimal Health:
Secrets To Holistic Healing

This book is a compilation of the author's personal experiences with different natural healing systems. It offers practical holistic approaches to restore and maintain your optimal health naturally.

A Shift Toward Purpose:
Secrets to an Amazing Career

When making decisions about a career, people often sabotage their own dreams with logical but futile "Yes, but…" kinds of self-talk. This book covers important factors to consider when making a career choice— especially a career change—from "Why this choice?" to "How to transition?" to "When to begin?"

A Shift Toward Love:
Secrets to Harmonious Relationships

This book covers a wide spectrum of your relation- ships—from the relationship with yourself to your partner, your ex, children, parents, siblings and friends. It candidly discusses practical ways to reclaim your wholeness and transform your relationship with.others.

Thank you for reading my book–I hope you enjoyed it!

Your review of the book is VERY important – it helps me create valuable content for my readers and clients. I would really appreciate it if you could go to the retailer where you purchased the book and write your review. Additionally, if you would like to receive a review copy of my next book in the "Dare to Change Life" series, please feel free to contact me here: **millenlivis.com/contact-2/** or email me directly at **millen@daretochangelife.com**

~ Millen Livis

NOTES

NOTES

NOTES

NOTES

NOTES

Dare
to Change
Life